## Introduction

This book is written as a guide to help you answer those burning questions you have.

I have to remind myself that this isn't a standard size. That I've made it smaller. I also need to add an empty pages. The page that they need to be visible on is always an odd page.

And on a happier note, I've actually sold a few of the paperback copies of my slipper book. So that's exciting. I also just realized that I have no idea how to format a book that contians regular writting. I've done patterns waaaay too long. Do peopel do indentations anymore?? Yes they do. I checked.

This book is for entertainment purposes only. ALL READINGS AND REPORTS ARE FOR ENTERTAINMENT PURPOSES ONLY AND

SHOULD NOT BE CONSTRUED AS MEDICAL, LEGAL OR FINANCIAL ADVICE ON ANY SUBJECT MATTER. THE PLATFORMS ARE PROVIDED "AS IS," "AS AVAILABLE," AND WITHOUT WARRANTIES OF ANY KIND. YOU USE THE PLATFORMS AT YOUR OWN SOLE RISK.

## How to Use This Book

I should probably have a little soemthing about how to use this book. And the inspiration behind it. Consulted tarot decks, the Tao and other sources to gather information and create the answers.

Don't do the formating until the entire intro is done. Why make more work for yourself if you don't have to.

4

*It takes dark to see the light.
Remember that nothing is
permanent.*

- 120 -

*Positive thoughts may make you feel better, but it won't influence the outcome.*

*- 134 -*

8

*You are at a fork in the road.
You must choose.*

*38*

10

*The reason for life events are not always clear.*

**125**

12

*You've done all you can.
Time to let the situation
run it's course.*

**113**

14

## 15

*Someone is withholding information.*

*230*

16

*There's more to this than what there appears to be.*

*250*

18

*Allow others to follow their calling so you can follow yours.*

*289*

20

*Now is not the time to make a decision.*

**36**

22

*Not everyone has your best interests in mind.*

**195**

24

Worrying is useless.
If you can change it, do so.
If you can't, stop thinking
about it.

**114**

26

The time has come to choose.
Think rationally and
realistically.

164

*You will not achieve the desired outcome.*

**186**

30

*Everyone has their limits.*
*Be mindful of yours.*

**147**

*Sometimes it's not about you.*

*279*

## 35

*There are risks involved.*

**199**

36

*More work is required.*

**145**

38

*Triumph!*
*Efforts will now manifest.*

**70**

40

*If any part of you feels positive about the outcome, then YES!*

**132**

42

*Not all is lost. Have hope.*

**159**

*The current situation has posed many challenges.*

**158**

*Choose the right moment.*
*You'll know when it's time.*

**115**

48

*Success is yours!*

**224**

50

*Take action where you can.*

**135**

*It is possible.*
*Focus your energies on the*
*desired outcome.*

**49**

54

*You need more information to make the correct decision.*

6

*Your greatest success occurs through helping others.*

**216**

58

*Your wish is granted.*

**90**

*Self-care is required.*

- 72 -

*Analyze your question with a more rational approach.*

**- 251 -**

*There is always light after
the darkest of storms.*

- 76 -

*No time like the present.*
*Act!*

- 274 -

*You are moving in the correct direction.*

- 54 -

*Allow it to happen.*
*No more effort is required.*

- 119 -

*Focus on the solution
to the problem,
not the problem itself.*

*- 273 -*

*Be wary when emotions run high.*

*- 266 -*

*Clear your mind.
Focus on your question
and ask again.*

*- 137 -*

*Make space for your
new beginning.*

- 264 -

*Power struggles and competition surround you.*

*- 85 -*

*Other factors are influencing the outcome.*

- 101 -

You've been through many hardships. You are stronger because of it.

- 241 -

*You have the skill and talent to bring about a successful conclusion.*

— 249 —

*Life moves in cycles.*
*What was is no more.*
*New begins again.*

*- 203 -*

*Trust your gut.*

*- 44 -*

92

*Your efforts will now bear fruit.*

*- 177 -*

*Everything will be fine
in the end.*

- 234 -

*Do what feels right regardless of the opinions of others.*

*- 236 -*

98

*Effort is unnecessary.*

- 123 -

100

All is as it should be.

- 225 -

*Quit "the grind"; even for a little while.*

- 181 -

*The outcome is uncertain.*

- 99 -

*Abundance! Victory! Success!*
*Everything positive is coming your way!*

*- 153 -*

*Yes!*

- 17 -

*Good ideas appear from nowhere.*

*- 93 -*

*These are trying times for you.*

- 157 -

*Like the seasons,
life is cyclical.*

- 121 -

*Being of service to others,
even for a moment,
benefits everyone.*

*- 280 -*

*Like attracts like.
Be what you want to
see around you.*

*- 136 -*

*Things may become difficult for you.*

*- 213 -*

*The decision is up to you
and ONLY you.*

- 238 -

*Others will see and honor your success.*

*- 96 -*

*Your efforts will go unrewarded.*

*- 109 -*

*Find your life path.*

*- 237 -*

*The answer is no.*
*(Is this answer you wanted?)*

- 112 -

*Your answer is on its way.
Be patient.*

− 39 −

*Karma will come into play.*

*- 84 -*

*Focus on the outcome to bring it to reality.*

*- 48 -*

*Things may not work out
in your favor.*

- 214 -

*Bad news is on its way.*

**- 226 -**

*A new partnership
or relationship is on
the horizon.*

- 34 -

*More is not always better.*

*- 189 -*

*Allow for change to occur.*

*- 238 -*

*Things will turn out
as they should.*

- 91 -

150

*Everything is about to fall into place.*

- 176 -

*Your talents draw success and abundance towards you.*

**- 222 -**

154

*Your intuition is correct.*

*- 45 -*

*Your creative energy and unique way of thinking get you the results you want.*

- 1 -

*You may not succeed if you take action at this time.*

*- 206 -*

*Unanswered questions weigh heavily upon you.*

*- 173 -*

*Take stock and reassess.*

*- 66 -*

*Apply your energy, creativity and enthusiasm to the result you desire.*

- 14 -

*Let your inner wisdom
be your guide.*

*- 290 -*

*Disappointment is a thing of the past.*

*- 202 -*

*Important facts are being withheld from you.*

- 183 -

172

*You will reap your just rewards.*

*- 139 -*

*You have inner strength.*

*- 240 -*

*If you don't try,
it won't happen.*

*- 27 -*

*You will get want you need,
not what you want.*

- 92 -

*Your question is valid.*
*Follow up on it.*

- 1 -

*Stay the course.*

*- 87 -*

*Don't believe everything you are told.*

*- 23 -*

*The darkness inspires our gratitude for the light.*

*- 130 -*

*Allow your life to
unfold effortlessly.*

- 25 -

Your load is heavy.
Be mindful of
your limitations.

- 144 -

*There is no change to your current situation.*

- 155 -

*Think creatively in regards to your desired outcome.*

- 4 -

*Focus on what is most important to you.*

*- 126 -*

Trust others so they,
in turn, can trust you.

- 288 -

200

*Consider the alternatives.*

*- 246 -*

*Be careful and take heed.*

- 196 -

*One phase of life is ending
so another can begin.*

*- 259 -*

206

*Accept the present moment.*

*- 284 -*

*Being grateful allows f or more blessings.*

- 268 -

*Almost there!  
Success is closer than  
you think.*

*- 142 -*

*You are healed  
of all troubles.*

*- 263 -*

214

*The answer is already evident.*

*- 61 -*

*Hold steadfast.*
*Focus on your goal.*

- 245 -

*Your efforts bring
abundance into your life.*

*- 207 -*

*A run of bad luck is about to befall you.*

*- 193 -*

*Don't give up.*
*You have the strength to*
*accomplish your goals.*

- 143 -

*You will hear many "no's" before you hear a "yes".*

*- 239 -*

*Your current situation is dragging you down. Take control and move forward.*

*- 262 -*

228

*Working too hard is as detrimental to you as not working hard enough.*

*- 209 -*

*What you currently have
no longer serves you.
A change is required.*

*- 260 -*

*Actions taken to control others never work.*

*- 287 -*

*Take the initiative.*
*Start now.*

— 1 —

*There will be change from the current situation.*

*- 149 -*

238

*Have faith.*

## - 21 -

*The reality
is not as frightening
as you imagine.*

*- 200 -*

*Look for
alternative solutions.*

- 8 -

*More action is required.*

*- 178 -*

*Follow through with what you think is correct.*

- 104 -

248

*A break is necessary.*

- 75 -

250

*Now is not the time to be overly emotional.*

- 252 -

*Be careful of who you trust.*

*- 231 -*

*Time has passed.
Are you where
you want to be?*

*- 55 -*

*Rose colored glasses make everything seem ok.*

**- 22 -**

258

*Partnerships and collaboration are needed to succeed.*

*- 30 -*

*As you sow,
so shall you reap.*

*- 267 -*

*New beginnings are in sight.*

- 148 -

*If you believe
you are worthy,
it will happen.*

*- 42 -*

*Following
your life path
may not appeal
to everyone.*

*- 235 -*

268

*You need to lose
in order to gain.*

**- 258 -**

270

*The answer requires a unique approach.*

− 13 −

*Look past the negative.
There is always a
ray of light.*

*- 102 -*

*Assess the situation from a different perspective.*

*- 3 -*

*Simplicity in life
grants untold freedom.*

*- 26 -*

278

*The work can wait.*

- 180 -

280

You shall reap
the rewards earned
through your hard work.

- 71 -

*Remove yourself from the situation.*

*- 88 -*

284

*Good news is on its way.*

- 218 -

*You are destined to have
the life you most desire.*

*- 127 -*

*You did everything you could. Manifesting your desire needs time.*

- 59 -

290

*Don't let fear stop you.
Be brave!*

*- 198 -*

*Quiet your mind*
*for a moment.*
*Think of nothing.*

*- 276 -*

Your heart will tell you
when the time is right.

- 269 -

*The only guarantee in life is change.*

**- 152 -**

*Your mind is leading you down a false path.*

*- 201 -*

300

*What once was gone
is making its way
back to you.*

- 162 -

*Sometimes you need to give in order to recieve.*

*- 278 -*

304

*Things are looking up for you!*

*- 190 -*

*Stand up for what you think is right.*

- 103 -

308

*Think carefully and reflect on the matter.*

- 255 -

*Relationships ebb and flow like waves on the ocean.*

*- 150 -*

*Your current environment leaves much to be desired. Time for change.*

- 165 -

*Reconnect with your purpose.*

- 128 -

*Stay humble.*
*Success, abundance*
*and greatness cannot*
*occur without the*
*help of others.*

- 89 -

*Work with what transpires around you.*

- 117 -

*Now is a great time to make a change.*

*- 223 -*

*Do NOT*
*take action now.*

*- 105 -*

*Indecision and doubt surrounds you.*

- 172 -

*Your situation will improve.*

- 191 -

328

*You will gain
your heart's desire.*

*- 167 -*

330

*Clear your mind.*
*Focus on your breathing*
*for 10 breaths.*
*Ask again.*

*- 271 -*

*Someone will share their knowledge with you.*

**- 220 -**

*The grass always appears greener on the other side.*

- 24 -

*The Universe
has you covered.
Don't worry.*

*- 40 -*

*Working with others will be beneficial.*

*- 31 -*

340

*No!*
*You have never been
more wrong.*

*- 47 -*

*Success is not guaranteed.*

*- 98 -*

*Do not expect charity
or help from others.*

**- 212 -**

*Options will present themselves in time. Choose wisely when they arrive.*

- 35 -

*You require balance
in your life.*

*- 208 -*

*Your efforts will be rewarded.*

- 169 -

352

*Life isn't always sunshine and roses.*

*- 129 -*

*You require a
fresh perspective.*

*- 257 -*

*A sudden and welcome change is about to occur.*

*- 247 -*

358

*You are about to go on a journey.*

- 192 -

360

*Approach this problem
from a different perspective.*

*- 7 -*

*Share your abundance
with others.*

**- 215 -**

*Stay calm.
It will work itself out.*

*- 106 -*

*Others may not have
your best interests at heart.*

*- 140 -*

368

*Do everything that you can without expecting a reward.*

- 124 -

370

*No!*

- 18 -

*Take the risk.*

*- 211 -*

374

*Things shall stay the course.*

*- 285 -*

*Spread your blessings through kind actions towards others.*

**- 217 -**

*You did all you can do.*

*- 74 -*

380

*You did your best.*
*Allow time for your desire to manifest.*

*- 58 -*

382

*You may not know
the whole truth.*

*- 182 -*

*Life changing
news is on its way.*

*- 227 -*

*Good things are coming your way.*

- 94 -

*The time has come to separate.*

*- 166 -*

*You are moving closer
to your goal.
Keep moving forward!*

- 57 -

*Things will not go as planned.*

- 68 -

394

*Take action
and begin today.*

- 2 -

*Anything is possible.*

*- 133 -*

*It will work itself out.*

*- 73 -*

400

*A positive energy surrounds you.*

*- 64 -*

*A mentor will appear
when the time is right.*

*- 221 -*

*You are the creator
of your destiny.
Take action.*

*- 43 -*

*Selfishness is
never rewarded.*

- 187 -

*Reconsider your desired outcome. Is this truly what you want?*

*- 52 -*

You require a
change of scenery.

- 254 -

*Collaborations are required for a positive outcome.*

*- 50 -*

*Better times are ahead.*

*- 265 -*

*Rethink your reasons for wanting what you want.*

*- 53 -*

418

*Focus on feeling good in your mind, body and soul.*

*- 270 -*

420

*Are your "facts" false conclusions?*

*- 243 -*

*Hard work is not always rewarded.*

- 122 -

*You know the answer.*

- 62 -

*Things are not always
what they seem.*

*- 107 -*

*The answer is unclear.*

*- 100 -*

430

*You have had some success.*
*Keep going!*

- 56 -

*Take time for yourself.*

**- 179 -**

*Your surroundings are about to change.*

*- 228 -*

*Justice will prevail.*

*- 256 -*

*Not everything resolves
as we would like.*

**- 185 -**

440

*Don't overextend yourself*

*- 146 -*

*If you don't choose,
it will be chosen for you.*

- 116 -

*Everything is moving towards a positive outcome.*

*- 67 -*

*The Divine
looks after all things.*

- 4 -

*It is up to you to
create the final result.*

*- 19 -*

*What is the lesson you need to learn?*

- 160 -

452

*Be mindful of your family and home.*

*- 233 -*

454

Failure teaches us what
NOT
to do in the future.

- 205 -

456

*Life changing events are about to occur.*

*- 229 -*

*You are separated from your desire.*

- 175 -

*Many options are available.
Choose with your heart.*

*- 163 -*

462

*Be mindful of
negative events, actions,
and situations.*

*- 197 -*

*Partnerships and mentors will help move this forward.*

- *253* -

*Be mindful of choosing the right moment.*

*- 282 -*

*Pay attention
to the details.*

**- 242 -**

*Things will start happening for you.*

- 108 -

*Might does not make right.*

*- 86 -*

*Compromise and group effort is necessary.*

*- 261 -*

*This too, shall pass.*

*- 131 -*

*Even in failure there are lessons to learn.*

- 97 -

480

*Life isn't always fair.*

- 194 -

*Listen to your inner voice.*
*It speaks the truth.*

*- 277 -*

484

*Go with the flow
and be open to
new possibilities.*

*- 118 -*

486

All in due time.
Good things are
on their way.

- 138 -

Things are about to
quickly change.

- 110 -

490

*Consider your
options carefully.*

*- 23 -*

*The mundane and everyday shall continue.*

- 154 -

494

*Negotiations are necessary to obtain the desired result.*

- 51 -

*Your optimism will effect the outcome.*

**- 29 -**

*You are ready for change.*
*Now it can begin.*

*- 248 -*

500

*Even in failure,
one can still succeed.*

*- 204 -*

502

There is more than
enough for everyone.

- 272 -

*Negative emotions engulf you.*

- 171 -

*Let events run their course.*
*You cannot effect the outcome.*

*- 33 -*

*There is great freedom in doing and having less.*

- 9 -

510

*You are in a period of transition.*

- 63 -

*Divine intervention has come into play.*

- 69 -

514

*You require more information.*

*- 37 -*

*Anger and frustration
threaten your
peace of mind.*

*- 174 -*

*Enjoy today,
but plan for tomorrow.*

- 219 -

*It will take effort to see the desired result.*

*- 28 -*

*The tallest nail is the one hammered down.*

- 20 -

524

*Leave the past behind.*
*Look towards the future.*

- 161 -

526

*The true motivations
negate the outcome.*

*- 18 -*

*Always wanting more
will ruin you.*

- 65 -

*Now is the time for careful consideration and rational thought.*

- 46 -

*Relationships
sprout, bloom and grow.*

- 151 -

*You MUST choose.*
*Take action to manifest*
*your choice.*

- 170 -

*Take time to reflect.*

— 210 —

*Emotions are at an all time high. Regain composure.*

*- 184 -*

*You will prevail.*

- 141 -

542

*Time to start over.*

*- 15 -*

*You are enough
as you are
RIGHT NOW.*

*- 286 -*

*Follow your heart
and ignore others' judgment
of your choices.*

*- 244 -*

*Change is coming,
but it will take time.*

- 111 -

550

*Be mindful.*
*Be present.*

*- 281 -*

552

*You are uncertain
of the outcome.*

**- 11 -**

*You will be satisfied with your accomplishments.*

*- 95 -*

*Time for change.*
*Are you ready?*

*- 156 -*

*Outside influence will impact the outcome.*

*- 32 -*

*What you've worked
hard to achieve, you'll receive.*

- 168 -

562

*Transition is scary.*
*You have the fortitude to persevere.*

*- 16 -*

Time will show
you the answer.

- 60 -

*Get out of your comfort zone and try something new.*

- 5 -

568

*When in doubt,
just...BE.*

*- 275 -*

# Notes

# Notes

# Notes

# Notes

# Notes

# Notes

# Notes

# Notes

# Notes

## Notes

# Notes

CPSIA information can be obtained
at www.ICGtesting.com
Printed in the USA
BVHW051533080623
665629BV00013B/220